WHO Am I?

Riddles for Kids

GAIL BOWLING

To order additional copies of this book, contact:
Xlibris
844-714-8691
www.Xlibris.com
Orders@Xlibris.com

ISBN: Softcover   978-1-6698-1666-9
         Hardcover   978-1-6698-1667-6
         EBook   978-1-6698-0763-6
Library of Congress Control Number: 2022905236
Print information available on the last page

Rev. date: 04/11/2022

I WORK WITHIN A CLASSROOM AND MOSTLY I JUST TALK
IF I NEED TO WRITE THINGS DOWN THEN OFTEN I USE CHALK

I LIKE TO MAKE FOLKS LOOK GOOD I CUT AND STYLE AND COMB
I LIKE FOR THEM TO LEAVE MY CHAIR LOOKING PRETTY TO GO HOME

I MOSTLY WORK WITH POTS AND PANS OR SKILLETS AND A STOVE
SOMETIMES I MIX UP GOOEY DOUGH AND TURN IT INTO LOAVES

I'M HIRED FOR CHILDRENS PARTIES TO DO TRICKS AND TWIST BALLOONS
I PAINT MY FACE AND WEAR WILD CLOTHES AND EVEN PLAY SOME TUNES

CLOWN

I CARRY FOOD TO TABLES ON MY ARM OR ON BIG TRAYS
FOLKS COME FOR ALL OCCASIONS AND ESPECIALLY FOR BIRTHDAYS

YOU SEE ME ON THE HIGHWAY MY RIG ROLLS MOST EVERYDAY
I SIT HIGHER THAN THE OTHER CARS AND SEE THINGS FAR AWAY

I WORK WHERE THERE ARE DOCTORS HEALING PEOPLE IS MY GAME
IF PATIENTS DON'T KNOW WHO I AM A TAG DISPLAYS MY NAME

I DRIVE A GIANT TRACTOR TO HARVEST CROPS WITHIN A FIELD
I PLANT AND GROW THEM CAREFULLY TO GET A BIGGER YIELD

I WORK WITH SHRUBS AND FLOWERS I PLANT AND WATCH THINGS GROW
ON HANDS AND KNEES I PLUCK THE WEEDS AND THEN IT'S OFF TO MOW

I CLIMB UP IN A BIG RED TRUCK WHEN THE SIREN BELLS ALARM
IF I DON'T LEAVE THE STATION FAST BUILDINGS COME TO HARM

I HANG OUT AT THE POOL IN SUMMER SITTING ON A TOWER
IF A SWIMMER NEEDS SOME HELP I SWIM WITH ALL MY POWER

I WORK INSIDE A BUILDING WITH MANY BOOKS UPON THE SHELVES
PEOPLE COME TO RESEARCH THINGS AND EDUCATE THEMSELVES

I CRUISE IN CARS WITH LIGHTS ON TOP TO PROTECT AND SERVE
SO PLEASE DRIVE VERY CAREFULLY SO YOU DON'T SPEED OR SWERVE

I SOAK HANDS AND TRIM LONG NAILS AND THEN I FILE AND POLISH
A BRIGHT SHINY COLOR ALWAYS MAKES GIRLS FEEL SO STYLISH

I DUST AND SCRUB AND VACUUM TO TIDY ALL I SEE
WHEN I FINISH WITH A ROOM IT'S AS CLEAN AS IT CAN BE

I SAIL THE MIGHTY OCEANS WITH A CREW THAT'S BRAVE AND STRONG
WE DOCK AT MANY PLACES BUT WE NEVER STAY TOO LONG

I WANDER WITH MY SHEEP ALL DAY ON FLATLANDS AND ON HILLS
WHEN THE SHEEP ARE TO BE SHORN THE WOOL'S SENT TO THE MILLS

I TAXI DOWN THE RUNWAY I NEED SPEED TO REACH THE SKY
IT TAKES A LOT OF SKILL TO MAKE THIS GIANT STEEL BIRD FLY

I PICK UP MANY PEOPLE AND TAKE THEM HERE AND THERE
I WILL KICK THEM OFF MY RIDE IF THEY DON'T PAY THEIR FARE

I'M USUALLY IN THE CIRCUS ON A WIRE HIGH AS I CAN GET
I HOLD A POLE FOR BALANCE SO I DON'T FALL INTO THE NET

Printed in the United States
by Baker & Taylor Publisher Services